I Want to Know™
About the HOLY SPIRIT

Rick Osborne and K. Christie Bowler

ZondervanPublishingHouse
Grand Rapids, Michigan

A Division of HarperCollins Publishers

10

For Lightwave
Managing Editor: Elaine Osborne
Art Director: Terry Van Roon

Photo on page 22 courtesy of Zondervan Publishing House.
The photos used on page 9, 16, and 28 were obtained from Corel Corporation's Professional Photo CD collection.
The images used on page 10, 16, 17, 18, 22, 23, and 24 were obtained from ISMI's Master Photos Collection, 1895 Francisco Blvd. East, San Rafael, CA 94901-5506, USA.

Library of Congress Cataloging-in-Publication Data

Osborne, Rick, 1961– .
    The Holy Spirit : who the Holy Spirit is, what He does, and how He works in me / Rick Osborne and K. Christie Bowler.
        p. cm.—(I want to know™)
    Summary: Introduces concepts for experiencing the Holy Spirit, developing a hunger and curiosity for God's work, and practicing the basic principles of Christian living. Includes cartoons, games, and activities.
    ISBN 0–310–22093–9 (hardcover)
    1. Holy Spirit—Juvenile literature. [1. Holy Spirit. 2. Christian life.] I. Bowler, K. Christie 1958– . II. Title. III. Series: Osborne, Rick, 1961– . I want to know™.
BT121.2.O74   1998
231'.3–dc21
                          98-4012
                          CIP
                          AC

Published by Zondervan Publishing House, Grand Rapids, Michigan 49530, U.S.A. http://www.zondervan.com

Printed in Mexico.

Building Christian faith in families
A Lightwave Production
P.O. Box 160 Maple Ridge, B.C., Canada V2X 7G1

98 99 00 /DR/ 5 4 3 2 1

Contents

28

11

13

Who Is the Holy Spirit?

A Real Live Ghost

Do you believe in ghosts? There's one ghost that's real. Any guesses? Jesus told his disciples or followers to baptize people in the name of the Father, Son, and Holy . . . Ghost! Well, okay, he's not really a ghost. He's a spirit, the *Holy Spirit.* And he's your best friend! You can learn about him in God's book, the Bible.

He Is God

That's the first thing to know. Awesome! We know he is God because:

The Bible says so: "Now the Lord is the Holy Spirit" (2 Corinthians 3:17). Also, a husband and wife sold their land and brought part of the money to Peter. They lied, saying they had brought all the money. Peter told them, "Satan . . . made you lie to the Holy Spirit. . . . You've lied to God" (Acts 5:3–4). Pretty clear, huh?

He has qualities only God has: He's *eternal*—no beginning or end. "He did this through the power of the eternal Holy Spirit" (Hebrews 9:14). He's *omnipresent*—present everywhere. "How can I get away from your Spirit? Where can I go to escape from you? If I go up to the heavens, you are there" (Psalm 139:7–8). He's *equal with God.* "Baptize them in the name of the Father and of the Son and of the Holy Spirit" (Matthew 28:19). There's only one God, but he is three equal persons—the Father, the Son, and the Holy Spirit. (See Matthew 3:16–17.)

He does things only God can do: He was involved in *creation.* "The Spirit of God was hovering over the waters" (Genesis 1:2). He helps people to be *born into God's kingdom.* "No one can enter God's kingdom without being born through . . . the Holy Spirit" (John 3:5). He *came from heaven.* "At that moment heaven was opened. Jesus saw the Spirit of God coming down on him like a dove" (Matthew 3:16).

He Is a Person

The Holy Spirit feels, thinks, and acts like a person: The Bible calls him *"he,"* never *"it."* "But when the Spirit of truth comes, *he* will guide you into all truth" (John 16:13). He *knows things.* "The Spirit understands all things" (1 Corinthians 2:10). He *gives gifts* and *makes decisions.* "All of the gifts are produced by one and the same Spirit. He gives them to each person, just as he decides" (1 Corinthians 12:11). He's a *friend.* "I will ask the Father. And he will give you another Friend to help you. . . . The Friend is the Spirit of Truth" (John 14:16–17). He *can be lied to.* Remember Acts 5? *He feels.* "Do not make God's Holy Spirit sad" (Ephesians 4:30).

Convinced? He's a person—kind of like us—and he's God—not at all like us. What an awesome Friend! Want to know more? Keep reading!

Names of the Holy Spirit

The Holy Spirit's names tell us about him.

The Spirit of the Lord: He's God's Spirit. He's powerful and can help us with our problems.

The Holy Spirit: He's holy or pure. There's nothing bad or wrong in him. He helps us to be pure.

Counselor: He's very wise. He gives great advice and he's on our side. He defends us.

Comforter: He knows our problems, hopes, dreams, and worries. He comforts us.

Spirit of Truth: He never lies. We can trust him just as we trust God.

Spirit of the Lord
Spirit of God
Counselor
Spirit of Truth
the Promise
Comforter
Spirit of Christ
The Spirit who testifies
The Eternal Spirit
Holy Ghost
The Spirit

The Holy Spirit's Story

You Are What You Do

Imagine trying to get to know a couch potato. There she sits. And sits. What do you know about her? Not much. But if she studies hard, cooks supper, and helps her dad wax the car, you know a lot more about her. People's actions show who they are. A great way to know the Holy Spirit is to see what he does. Read the New Testament and you'll see him at work right away!

The Holy Spirit came on Mary so she'd have God's Son, Jesus. The Spirit came on Jesus like a dove when he was baptized. He anointed Jesus—he guided and filled him with everything he needed in order to do what God wanted. Jesus said, "The Spirit of the Lord is on me. He has anointed me to tell the good news to poor people, announce freedom for prisoners,

[make] the blind see again, free those who are beaten down, and announce the year when he will set his people free" (Luke 4:18–19). Later, before Jesus was killed, he told his disciples, "I will ask the Father. And he will give you another Friend to help you and to be with you forever. The Friend is the Spirit of truth" (John 14:16–17). Jesus told them to wait for the Holy Spirit.

Powerful Promise

A few weeks later, at the Feast of Pentecost, "a sound came from heaven. It was like a strong wind blowing. It filled the whole house. [The disciples] saw something that looked like tongues of fire separate and settle on each of them. All of them were filled with the Holy Spirit" (Acts 2:2–4). They were filled with courage and

The Holy Spirit worked through people and helped them do all kinds of things like make art, defeat their enemies, build, do miracles, and more.

told everyone about Jesus and what had happened. God had promised this would happen hundreds of years before when he said, "After that, I will pour out my Spirit on all people" (Joel 2:28–29).

That was the beginning! The Holy Spirit had come to help all Jesus' followers obey God and spread the good news. He helped them do miracles, including healing and raising people from the dead! He guided and changed them. That's his main job—to make Jesus' followers more like Jesus.

Long Ago

The Holy Spirit didn't start his work with Jesus. He's been around since the beginning. In the Old Testament he came on people and helped them obey God. For example, God chose Bezalel to make a meeting place for him. He said, "I have filled him with the Spirit of God, with skill, ability and knowledge in all kinds of crafts" (Exodus 31:3). He also came on leaders and helped them defeat Israel's enemies. He came on King David with power. He spoke to prophets, gave Daniel wisdom, and helped Zerubbabel rebuild the temple.

God's Spirit in the Old Testament

Creation: He was there when the world began (Genesis 1:2).

Art: He helped people do beautiful artistic work (Exodus 31:3–6).

Leadership: God put his Spirit on seventy elders so they could help Moses lead the people (Numbers 11:16–17).

Kings: He came on Saul and David after Samuel anointed them to be kings (1 Samuel 10:10; 2 Samuel 6:13).

Prophecy: He gave prophets the words to speak God's message (Ezekiel 2:2).

What Is He Like?

Grumpy or Happy?

Uh-oh! Here comes Grumpy George! He's working hard. He's even doing a good job—but he's frowning, whining, and complaining. Why is he called Grumpy George? Because how people do things tells us a lot about them.

We know the Holy Spirit is excellent at getting God's stuff done. But what's he *like?* Well, the Holy Spirit is God. That means he's like God. So, if we know God, we'll know his Spirit. First off, God is *love*—so is the Holy Spirit. That means the Spirit's attitude to everything he does comes from love. He does all his work with a smile and a song!

Great Qualities!

He's holy: This seems obvious! He is pure and perfect. Also, part of his job is to make us holy or "set apart" for God. That means he helps us do what's right (obey and serve God) and be good people (kind, gentle, and loving). Put that together with his love, and we know he'll help us if we blow it!

He's gentle: "Don't put out the Holy Spirit's fire" (1 Thessalonians 5:19). This means we *can* put his fire out. We can squelch the Holy Spirit and stop him from working! He'll never force us. He wants us to work *with* him. Jesus said, "Come to me, all you who are tired. I will give you rest. I am gentle and free of pride" (Matthew 11:28–29).

He's emotional: He has feelings. His heart is open to us because he loves us. He pours God's love into us

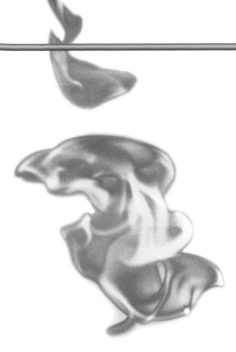

(Romans 5:5) and gives us joy (1 Thessalonians 1:6). But we can resist and oppose him (Acts 7:51) and make him sad (Ephesians 4:30). Because he has emotions, we know that he understands ours.

He's selfless: He doesn't want people to focus on him. He came to focus us on Jesus. You know people you just want to be around? People you're drawn to? The Holy Spirit draws us to Jesus. He shows us how

wonderful Jesus is and makes us want to know him more.

The Holy Spirit is great! He's someone we want to be around and know!

Symbols of the Holy Spirit

The Bible uses several pictures or symbols to help us understand what the Holy Spirit is like and what he does.

Dove: Doves are gentle and harmless. After Jesus' baptism, the Holy Spirit came on him like a dove.

Oil: People used to be "anointed" with oil. Pouring oil on them showed they had been chosen for a special task. The Spirit in our lives sets us aside for God.

Fire: The Holy Spirit came at Pentecost with "flames of fire." Fire cleans. The Holy Spirit burns or cleans out of us things God doesn't like—things that hurt and destroy our lives.

Water: Water makes things grow. Jesus called the Spirit "living water." He becomes a spring of eternal life inside us.

Wind: He came with a sound like a big wind! "Spirit" also means "breath" or "wind." Even though we can't see the wind, we can see what it does. It's the same with the Holy Spirit. He's real!

The Holy Spirit and Us

Ultimate Uncle

The Holy Spirit is wonderful. But what does that mean to you? Everything!

Imagine having a fantastic uncle who knows everything about everything, understands you completely, is a fantastic teacher, and loves every single thing about you. You can talk to him about anything! *And* he can do just about anything he wants. Would you hang out with him? Absolutely!

The Holy Spirit is like that uncle— only more fantastic! Here's what he does for us.

A caterpillar is "born again" as a butterfly. We're "born again" too when the Holy Spirit comes into our lives.

The Problem

Before we meet Jesus, it's like we're asleep—only we don't know it. The Holy Spirit wakes us up. He helps us recognize the bad things we do and shows us we need God. You see, God created us to be his children. He wanted to be our loving Father and live with us forever. But the first people, Adam and Eve, disobeyed God and sinned. Everyone who came after them sinned, too (Romans 3:23). Sin separates us from God—and the punishment is death. No matter what we do, we can't please God on our own. So everyone has to die for their sins (Romans 6:23).

The Answer

Jesus is the only person who never sinned! He died to pay for *our* sins (Colossians 1:13–14, 21–22). We just have to accept what he did. Jesus promised that when he went back to heaven he would send us another Friend to help us and be with us forever. That Friend, the Holy Spirit, came at Pentecost and fulfilled Jesus' promise. When people came running to see what was going on, Peter

When the Holy Spirit came, the disciples saw tongues of fire.

The Holy Spirit at Work

Drawing: One day the Holy Spirit told Philip, a church leader, to go for a walk. He met an Ethiopian reading the Bible. The Holy Spirit was drawing the Ethiopian to God. He told Philip to talk to him. The Ethiopian asked about the part of the Bible he was reading. Philip explained it was about Jesus. The man believed and was saved and baptized (Acts 8:26–40)!

Saving: As Cornelius, a Roman commander, was praying, an angel told him to send for Peter. The Holy Spirit told Peter to go with Cornelius's messengers. When Peter told Cornelius's family about Jesus, the Holy Spirit came on all of them. They were saved and baptized (Acts 10)!

Cornelius and his family believed Peter's message.

explained what had happened. They asked what to do and he said, "Turn away from your sins and be baptized in the name of Jesus Christ. Then your sins will be forgiven. You will receive the gift of the Holy Spirit" (Acts 2:38). The Spirit draws us to Jesus. He shows us we're guilty of sin. Then he shows us what God wants and helps us realize we need Jesus.

All we have to do is believe and ask God to forgive us and make us his children. The result? It's done. That means "he saved us by washing away our sins. We were born again. The Holy Spirit gave us new life. God poured out the Spirit on us freely because of what Jesus Christ our Savior has done" (Titus 3:5–6). When we pray and make this decision, the Holy Spirit comes into our lives. We're never alone again. You can't get any better than that! It's the beginning of a lifelong adventure!

The Holy Spirit Changes Us

Before he met Jesus, Saul hated Christians. He arrested them and had them beaten.

Jesus appeared to Saul, and Saul was blinded for three days.

Then Saul became a Christian himself and, as the apostle Paul, loved and helped many Christians.

Puppy or Guard Dog?

What now? Jesus died for us and the Holy Spirit is in us. Is that it? Nope. We don't just wake up perfect the next day. Take puppies. They're not born full-grown. They're born as cuddly furballs that can only eat and crawl. They can't fetch newspapers, no matter how hard they try. But we train them as they grow and they become good fetchers and good buddies.

We're not born full-grown Christians, either. We have to "grow up." Before Jesus, people's hearts were separated from God because of sin. No matter how they tried, they couldn't be who God wanted. But God promised, "I will give you a new spirit that is faithful to me. I will put my Spirit in you. I will move you to follow my rules" (Ezekiel 36:26–27). When Jesus came, he took care of sin. The separation is over! Now his Spirit joins us to God, just as God promised.

Saved and Sealed

"When you believed, he marked you with a seal. The seal is the Holy Spirit" (Ephesians 1:13). "He put his Spirit in our hearts and marked us as his own" (2 Corinthians 1:22). The seal shows that we belong to God. The Spirit works inside us, making us more and more God's, just as God promised!

God doesn't want us to obey him because he likes rules or "he said so." Everything he wants us to do comes from his love. He made the world. He knows it works a certain way. When we live in line with how it works, life is great. God wants us to have great lives so he tells us how to live. Jesus is the only one who ever lived life the way it was designed. So "God planned that those he had chosen would become like his Son" (Romans 8:29)—loving and obedient. That's the Spirit's job. "God is working in you" (Philippians 2:13). "We are being changed to become more like [Jesus]" (2 Corinthians 3:18).

Changed by Love

How does he do it? Think about the puppy. The more time we spend with our puppy, the better trained he becomes. He gets to know us and our rules. The Holy Spirit teaches us and helps us pray, understand the Bible, change our hearts, and get to know God. As we grow in our relationship with God—spend time with him, read the Bible, discover what he's like—we trust him more. We realize everything he does and asks is out of love. It's easy to obey someone who loves us. The Holy Spirit's focus is helping us understand this love. Obeying the rules doesn't change us. God's relationship with us makes the difference. We're changed by love!

Trust in Love

Do puppies get discouraged when they wet the floor one more time? Naw. They don't think about it. But we think about how we're doing. It's easy to look at our mistakes and think, *I'll never be who God wants me to be.*

STOP!

You've forgotten the Holy Spirit! You're trying to do it yourself. And that leads . . . nowhere! God gave us the Holy Spirit *because* we couldn't please him on our own. Mistakes are learning times. Take a break and remember: God *is* working in you. He *is* growing you. That's a fact. Count on it, and trust his love.

Spiritual Growth Chart

12 I'm obeying God more and more.

11 I'm getting to know God.

10 I begin to learn and change.

9 I join the church.

8 I'm serious.

7 NEW CHRISTIAN!

6 I'm sorry. Forgive me.

5 I'll make a decision.

4 I'm a sinner. I need help!

3 I understand what Jesus did.

2 I've heard of Jesus.

1 There is a God.

The Holy Spirit Helps Us

Paraclete—Hands-on Helper

How does the Holy Spirit work in our lives? Remember learning to bat? Your coach probably stood behind you, put his hands over yours, and swung with you. That's what the Holy Spirit does. He comes alongside us and puts his hands on ours. Sometimes we can sense him working and directing us. Sometimes we can't. That's okay. He's working anyway. Jesus called him the *paraclete*—a Greek word meaning several things:

Helper: Think of a good friend mixed with a great coach. He's for us, cheering us on. He helps us pray, and he defends us from our enemy, Satan. He gives us strength to make right choices and helps us know what to do in difficult situations. He helps us obey God, be kind, do our chores well, have good attitudes, find friends, and more. He's on our side—forever! "Since God is on our side, who can be against us?" (Romans 8:31). What's our part? Ask for God's help and trust that the Holy Spirit is on the job.

Comforter: You feel safe with your parents. When you're hurt or confused, you go to them for comfort. Jesus' disciples felt that way about Jesus. But he was leaving! Before he went, he promised to send them another Friend and Comforter. The Holy Spirit would take Jesus' place.

We *go to* our parents or a friend for comfort. We need to *go to* God, too. Doing that is simple! When we need encouragement or comfort, we choose to trust God and believe he's taking care of us. (We can ask for his help with that, too.) Then we ask him to comfort us. "Don't worry about anything. Instead, tell God about everything. Ask and pray. Give thanks to him. Then God's peace will watch over your hearts and your minds because you belong to Christ Jesus" (Philippians 4:6–7).

Teacher: Remember your *best* teacher? He or she made learning interesting, fun, and challenging. The Holy Spirit is even better! Jesus said, "The Holy Spirit will teach you all things" (John 14:26). "When the Spirit of truth comes, he will guide you into all truth" (John 16:13). "You don't need anyone to teach you. God's Spirit teaches you about everything" (1 John 2:27). God invented learning and teaching, so he knows the best ways to help us understand. And he makes it fun. (He invented fun, too.) When we're confused or don't understand, we simply ask God to teach us. He will!

Counselor: Say you have a problem. Where do you go? You look for someone wise—a counselor, aunt, uncle, pastor, or teacher. They help you think through the situation and make a good choice.

The Holy Spirit helps us make wise choices, often using the Bible. When we go to him knowing he has the answers, he'll show us what different passages mean. When we're in a situation and ask for wisdom and help, he'll remind us what we've learned and show us how to apply it. We just believe, ask, and act. He's interested in every part of our lives. There's nothing too complicated or insignificant for him to handle!

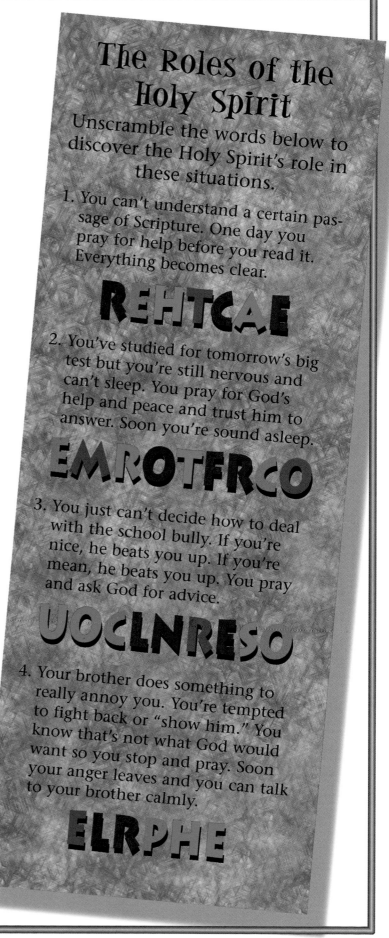

The Roles of the Holy Spirit

Unscramble the words below to discover the Holy Spirit's role in these situations.

1. You can't understand a certain passage of Scripture. One day you pray for help before you read it. Everything becomes clear.

REHTCAE

2. You've studied for tomorrow's big test but you're still nervous and can't sleep. You pray for God's help and peace and trust him to answer. Soon you're sound asleep.

EMROTFRCO

3. You just can't decide how to deal with the school bully. If you're nice, he beats you up. If you're mean, he beats you up. You pray and ask God for advice.

UOCLNRESO

4. Your brother does something to really annoy you. You're tempted to fight back or "show him." You know that's not what God would want so you stop and pray. Soon your anger leaves and you can talk to your brother calmly.

ELRPHE

The Fruit of the Spirit

Choose Your Fruit

The Spirit helps us grow, but into what?

Ever watched fruit grow? The flower becomes a bud, an unripe fruit, then a delicious one. It needs to be cared for, watered, and given time to grow. What the fruit is depends on the tree. Seems obvious! The Bible says we grow fruit! Not fruit to eat—character fruit. We bear bad fruit when we do only what we want—we're filled with jealousy, anger, and selfishness. Or we can bear good fruit when we do what God wants, letting his Spirit work in our hearts. "The fruit the Holy Spirit produces is love, joy and peace. It is being patient, kind, good, . . . faithful and gentle and having control of oneself" (Galatians 5:22–23).

Love: God is love. When his Spirit lives in us, so does love. The Spirit helps us love God with all of who we are, and love others as much as we love ourselves. Only God grows this love. Read 1 Corinthians 13!

Joy: "The joy of the Lord makes you strong" (Nehemiah 8:10). Joy doesn't mean always being happy or getting what we want. It's based on who God is. That doesn't change! Paul and Silas were beaten and imprisoned. But at midnight they were singing (Acts 16:25–34). That's joy!

Peace: "God's peace can never be completely understood" (Philippians 4:7). Inside us we have a deep peace from knowing God is in charge, and it comes out in how we treat and respond to others. God is taking care of everything. He loves us. No worries (Philippians 4:11–13)!

Jesus called us vines. We grow when we stick with God.

Patience: "Love is patient" (1 Corinthians 13:4). God never gives up on us or gets impatient. His patience helps us be patient. When others are mean, unkind, or rude, we treat them with respect and patience—just as God treats us (Psalm 37:7).

Kindness: We want good things for everyone—even those who aren't nice to us. We treat others kindly. We're helpful and considerate. God kindly saved us when we didn't know or love him (Titus 3:4–7). Everything we do and say should be kind!

Goodness: We don't just feel good, we do something about it. We serve others. "Barnabas was a good man. He was full of the Holy Spirit and of faith" (Acts 11:24). His goodness made people want to know Jesus! It also sent him to find Paul when others were afraid (Acts 11:25–26).

Faithfulness: We're loyal, keep our promises, and do what we say. People know they can rely on us. As a slave, Joseph worked faithfully even when he was put in jail (Genesis 39–41)!

Gentleness: This isn't being a wimp! Jesus was no wimp. It means treating people well no matter what. It's love in the little things—saying, "Excuse me," "Please," and "Thank you." If we're gentle, we aren't rude or angry. Check out Jesus' gentleness in John 8:1–11!

Self-Control: We control our thoughts, words, wants, and temper—they don't control us. We're disciplined. Self-control is powerful! "It is better to control your temper than to take a city" (Proverbs 16:32). Learning self-control is like training to be a star athlete (1 Corinthians 9:24–27).

Let's work with the Holy Spirit to grow this fruit in our lives by coming to God, asking him for it, and doing what he wants. We won't regret it!

As grape vines produce grapes, the Holy Spirit will produce his fruit in our lives.

The Holy Spirit Leads Us

Every Step

Would your parents point the way to Alaska, send you off, then check on you in five hours? There are so many turns, chances are you'd be lost. No. They'd bundle you into the car, check the map, and set off. The only way to get to Alaska a week from now is to take the right turns today.

God doesn't leave us alone for weeks at a time and then check on us. The Holy Spirit is not just doing mysterious things we hardly notice until months have passed. He knows we'll get there only if he leads us every step. He loves us so much he wants to be involved in every minute of our day!

Outside Leading

God uses many things and people to guide us.

The Bible: It's full of wisdom. The Holy Spirit helped people write the Bible—he can certainly help us understand it and know how to apply it!

People: Other Christians help us with tough decisions. But if they're worried about your choice, hold off!

Circumstances: As we trust God, things happen. We make the drama team. We get yard work that helps us save money for camp. Keep your eyes open and go for it!

Inside Leading

Peace and confidence: God is listening to our prayers. Sometimes he answers right away. Often his answer is quiet: We get the feeling we should do *this* instead of that. Our worry leaves. We become peaceful and confident.

Conscience: Everyone has a sense of right and wrong. The Holy Spirit just turns up the volume. Is it wrong to take something no one is using? Our conscience says to ask first. After all, it belongs to someone else.

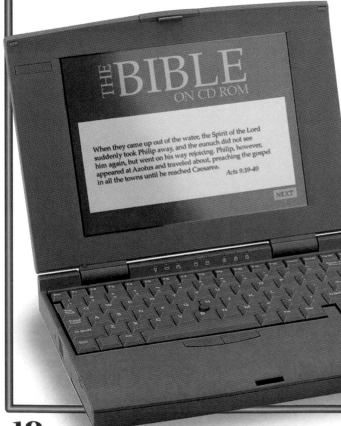

When they came up out of the water, the Spirit of the Lord suddenly took Philip away, and the eunuch did not see him again, but went on his way rejoicing. Philip, however, appeared at Azotus and traveled about, preaching the gospel in all the towns until he reached Caesarea. *Acts 9:39-40*

There are all kinds of Bibles available today, including computer Bibles. The Holy Spirit can use any of them to guide us.

Prompting: This is a very quiet feeling that we should do or say something. The Spirit knows what's coming. He knows when our friend needs an encouraging word, or when our help will make a difference in someone's day. When we find out what the Holy Spirit has done through us, we feel great!

Listening to the Spirit's quiet leading takes practice. The more we do it, the easier it gets to recognize and obey him. A lifetime of adventure awaits!

Dramatic Leading

Sometimes the Holy Spirit leads so dramatically that there's no doubt he's working!

Pillars of cloud and fire: When the Israelites traveled in the desert, "by day the Lord went ahead of them in a pillar of cloud. At night he led them with a pillar of fire" (Exodus 13:21–22).

A dry sea: God told Moses, "Hold your wooden staff . . . out over the Red Sea to part the water. Then the people can go through the sea on dry ground" (Exodus 14:16). It happened!

Animal vision: God showed Peter some "unclean" animals that Jews never ate and said to eat them. He did this to show Peter that God also loves non-Jews (whom Jews avoided like the unclean animals).

Taken Away: Philip obeyed God, met an Ethiopian, led him to Jesus, and baptized him. "When they came up out of the water, the Spirit of the Lord suddenly took Philip away" (Acts 8:39)! This is a little unclear, but many people think Philip vanished as God's Spirit carried him away!

When an Ethiopian wanted to know about Jesus, the Holy Spirit led Philip to him.

The Holy Spirit Works Through Us

Practice to Play

Why does the Holy Spirit work so hard to change us? Picture this: You're taking music. You practice, go to lessons, and become a wonderful musician. But you never play for anyone! Your skill is wasted unless others can enjoy it.

The Holy Spirit changes us for our sakes, but there's more to it than that. Oh, he loves us. Like the music teacher, he'd work in us just for us. But he knows it's more fun and fulfilling to let others enjoy the results. He wants to work through us to help others.

The more we become like Jesus, the more we want to act like him and be useful and encourage others. But we have enough trouble knowing how to solve *our* problems; how can we help others with theirs? Well, God knows everything! And he knows everyone inside out. He'll help us.

Be Filled

In fact, God planned for that. He wants us to *know* we need his help, be thirsty for more of him, and come to him. The Bible says to keep on being filled with the Holy Spirit. God wants us to ask for more and more of his Spirit. When we're ready to surrender our whole lives to God, we can pray and tell him that.

Our prayer might be: "Dear Father, I love you. Thanks for loving me and giving me your Spirit to help

From the time he was a boy, the prophet Samuel was led by the Holy Spirit.

John the Baptist was a prophet who was filled with the Holy Spirit from birth!

The Holy Spirit led Philip along a road so he could talk to an Ethiopian.

The Holy Spirit helped Peter do miracles and told Peter to share the good news of Jesus with non-Jews.

me know you and grow. I want to know you more. I need your help to live as you want and to help others. Please fill me full with your Spirit as the Bible says. Give me everything I need to do what you want. Thank you. In Jesus' name, amen."

You can be sure God will answer that prayer! He's got loads of good things for us to do. He prepared them long ago. But we can't do them alone. "The Holy Spirit is given to each of us in a special way. That is for the good of all" (1 Corinthians 12:7). He helps us.

So give your life completely to God. He'll fill you with his Spirit. Then hold on tight!

Speaking in Tongues

When the Holy Spirit filled people in the Bible, they often spoke in languages or "tongues" they didn't know! It happened at Pentecost. The listeners understood those languages. They asked, "Aren't all these people from Galilee? Why, then, do we each hear them speaking in our own native language?" (Acts 2:7–8). The same thing happened when the Holy Spirit came on Cornelius's family while Peter was preaching to them (Acts 10:44–48).

Sometimes *no one* can understand the languages! "Those who speak in languages they had not known before do not speak to people. They speak only to God. In fact, no one understands them" (1 Corinthians 14:2).

Today, there are some Christians who speak in tongues. Others don't. The Bible gives quite a few examples of Christians praying in tongues. But it doesn't say that every Christian should speak in tongues. The main thing is to seek God, follow his Spirit, and let him do whatever he wants in our lives!

God Has Good Things for You to Do!

The Holy Spirit helps ordinary people to be missionaries in other countries, help cheer up orphans, and even build homes for poor people.

The Holy Spirit and the Church

Church musicians play thier part in a worship service.

Find Your Place

Would a band leader train only the trumpet player? No. She also works with the whole band, forming them into a team that makes beautiful music together. The Holy Spirit doesn't work only in us, either. He's working in every Christian individually *and* all Christians as a whole. In fact, he links us together into the body of Christ, the church.

So when Christians come together, "the Holy Spirit makes you one in every way. So try your best to remain as one. Let peace keep you together. There is one body. There is one Spirit. . . . But each of us has received a gift of grace, just as Christ wanted us to have"

(Ephesians 4:3–4, 7). If we're all one, it makes sense to work together and look after each other. God gives each one something the body needs. If we don't do our part, who will?

Leaders' Part

Jesus, through his Spirit, "gave some the gift to be apostles, some the gift to be prophets, some the gift of preaching the good news, and some the gift to be pastors and teachers. He did it so that they might prepare God's people to serve. If they do, the body of Christ will be built up" (Ephesians 4:11–12). Our leaders prepare us to accomplish God's plan.

If you love baking, share your goodies with others.

For example, the pastor spends time studying for and praying about his sermon so he'll teach only what the Spirit wants. When he starts speaking, the Spirit helps him. He also helps us understand. It's the same with the musicians. They practice and pray for God's help to lead us in praise and worship. They prepare their hearts, too. The Spirit answers their prayers and draws us to God. He works in every part of the service, from offering to Sunday school. Nothing is wasted if we're open and ready to learn and meet God. That's our part.

Our Part

We should pray for the service, our pastor and leaders, and for God to teach us and meet with us. Then we come expecting something great, ready to receive whatever God has. Our faith increases—and God is free to work!

We should also come with our eyes open. What does God have for me today? Does someone need to be encouraged? Can I make someone smile? Where can I help out? If we have this attitude, we'll find a place to chip in and do our part. And the body is built up and encouraged. Awesome!

If you're good with little kids, help in the nursery.

Get Involved!

A church has lots of needs. Think of everything that has to be done at home. There are the physical chores—cleaning, cooking, taking out the garbage, and cutting the grass. And there's the relational stuff—getting along, working together, encouraging each other, obeying parents, helping siblings, being kind, and listening. It's the same at church, only more so!

You're needed! You can help with the physical needs, like cleaning floors, setting up chairs, tidying classrooms, or painting. You can bake for special events or wash cars to raise money. You can also help with the spiritual, relational stuff—help out in the nursery, assist a teacher, pray for the leaders, write thank-you notes, share what God does for you, and make new people feel welcome. Be creative! Your talents and gifts are needed!

If you're artistic, you can make signs and banners.

God-Given Talents

Designer Gifts

Whoopee! A gift! Don't you love gifts? They're wrapped up, free, no-strings-attached surprises. Because they're bought especially for you, they suit you. The better the buyer knows you, the better the gift matches you. Guess who knows us best of all? God! The Holy Spirit gives us gifts that perfectly match who God made us to be. The only string attached is to use them.

God knew long before you were born what you would be like. In fact, he designed you. He had a plan for your life and gave you strengths and talents so you'd fit his plan perfectly. To help you fulfill the plan, he gave you gifts—like being great at explaining things, leading, helping others, or using your hands. Whatever your gift, it's in the plan!

Gifted on Purpose

The plan includes our place in the body of Christ. God wants us to do a certain job in the church—our *calling.* He gives us the gifts we need to do it well. God's plan and our calling, gifts, and talents all work together and suit who he made us to be. Every Christian has a gift especially designed to strengthen and build up Jesus' body. "We are many persons. But in Christ we are one body. And each part of the body belongs to all the other parts. *We all have gifts.* They differ in keeping with the grace that God has given each of us" (Romans 12:5–6). These gifts line up with who God made us.

For example, the apostle Paul was created a certain way—he was a strong leader, a good speaker and teacher, and not afraid to act. As he grew in his faith, Paul started to act on the calling God had given him to take the good news of Jesus to non-Jews. To do that he used those same gifts and talents—he became a great leader in the body and spoke to thousands about Jesus. Even beatings and prison couldn't stop him from acting! God's job for Paul perfectly matched who Paul was.

How many Bible stories that involve the works or acts of the Holy Spirit can you find in this picture?

Put Them Together

What does that mean to you? Discover God's gift and what you're called to do. Pray about it. Ask those who know you for help. You can't know if you're good at something by thinking. I might *think* I'm a great basketball player, but I'll never *know* until I get on the court. And remember, we can grow. I won't get a three-pointer the first time I throw a basketball. But if I practice, I might! As we grow and learn, what we do will change. A doctor isn't always a doctor. She might start out sweeping floors to pay for school. At first we won't be excellent at what God has called us to do. But we can learn and grow.

The purpose of God's gifts is to help his body. Whatever talent God has given us, God can't use it if we keep it to ourselves. When we bring it to God and ask him to help us use it for him, he'll increase it! Not only will our church benefit—our whole lives will. Living as God wants affects other areas of our lives—school, jobs, relationships. It's all connected when God is in charge!

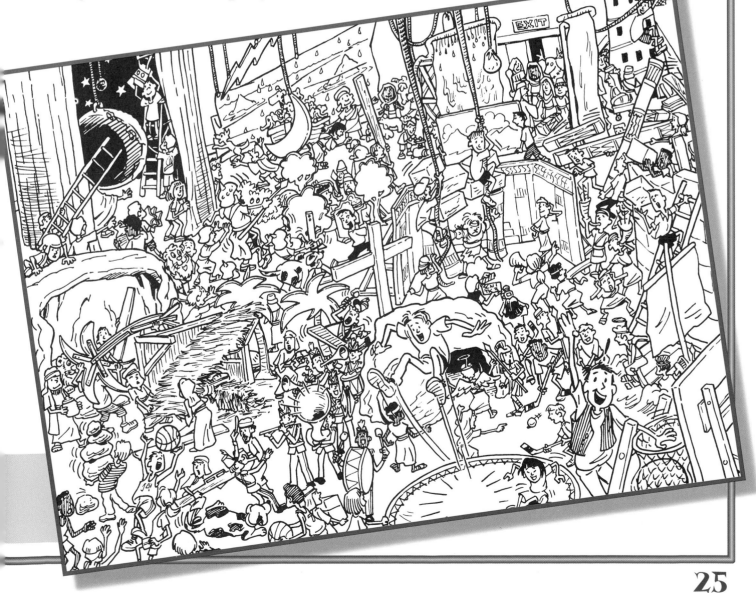

Gifts of the Spirit

For Love

The Holy Spirit can give us gifts that aren't natural to us as we need them for particular situations. He's always with us. He'll give whatever we need at the time to get the job done. The Bible talks about a lot of these gifts. All must be used in love. If there's no love, how can the gift build people up? The gifts are for others. God gives a gift to us for someone else who needs it. Now and then, when the Spirit decides, we get to work with God, showing his love for others through a gift he gives us. Now *that's* exciting!

Here are the gifts from 1 Corinthians 12:8–11. Churches have different ideas about how they work. The main thing is to listen to God and follow his Spirit.

Knowing Gifts

Word of knowledge: The Spirit gives us knowledge we couldn't know by ourselves. Jesus looked into a tree at a stranger and said, "Zacchaeus, come down at once" (Luke 19:5). Jesus knew his name!

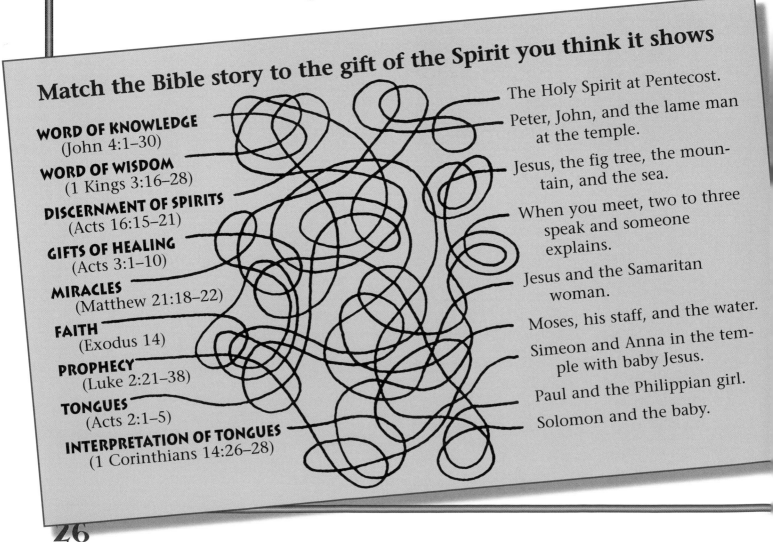

Match the Bible story to the gift of the Spirit you think it shows

WORD OF KNOWLEDGE
(John 4:1–30)

WORD OF WISDOM
(1 Kings 3:16–28)

DISCERNMENT OF SPIRITS
(Acts 16:15–21)

GIFTS OF HEALING
(Acts 3:1–10)

MIRACLES
(Matthew 21:18–22)

FAITH
(Exodus 14)

PROPHECY
(Luke 2:21–38)

TONGUES
(Acts 2:1–5)

INTERPRETATION OF TONGUES
(1 Corinthians 14:26–28)

The Holy Spirit at Pentecost.

Peter, John, and the lame man at the temple.

Jesus, the fig tree, the mountain, and the sea.

When you meet, two to three speak and someone explains.

Jesus and the Samaritan woman.

Moses, his staff, and the water.

Simeon and Anna in the temple with baby Jesus.

Paul and the Philippian girl.

Solomon and the baby.

Word of wisdom: Sometimes the Spirit gives us wisdom about what to do in a situation—wisdom we wouldn't have ourselves. This gift often helps us apply the Bible. Peter showed the religious leaders how Psalm 118:22 spoke of Jesus. The leaders knew Peter was uneducated and they were amazed (Acts 4:11–13)!

Discernment of spirits: This gift tells us whether something is from God, a person's own mind and heart, or evil spirits. Jesus knew that a man who said, "You are the Holy One of God," was saying it from an evil spirit (Mark 1:23–28).

Doing Gifts

Gifts of healing: These are gifts given to us for sick people. We pray for the sick—and they get well! People brought their sick into the streets so Peter's shadow would fall on them. They were healed (Acts 5:12–16)!

Miracles: Miracles are things impossible for us to do on our own. Jesus turned water into wine (John 2:1–11). Paul caused an evil man to go blind (Acts 13:4–12).

Faith: God gives us the ability to trust him when times are tough. Noah believed there would be a flood. He worked for years to build the ark because of his faith (Genesis 6–8).

John the Baptist had the gift of prophecy. He said about Jesus, "He will baptize you with the Holy Spirit" (Matthew 3:11).

Speaking Gifts

Prophecy: This is a message God gives to encourage people, make them stronger, and give them hope and comfort (1 Corinthians 14:3). Agabus prophesied a famine was coming (Acts 11:27–30). People responded by sending food and money to help. Talk about comforting!

Tongues: The Spirit gives us the ability to speak a language we haven't learned and don't understand. When Peter told Cornelius and his family about Jesus, the Holy Spirit came on them and gave them this gift (Acts 10:44–48).

Interpretation of tongues: When the gift of tongues is used in public meetings, it needs to be interpreted. With this gift someone gives the sense of what was said in tongues so everyone can benefit from it (1 Corinthians 14:27–28).

All these gifts make the body of Christ stronger. We should be open to receiving the Spirit's gifts and following where he leads. They're a natural part of being a Christian. God leads us closer to him and each other and gives us everything we need. What more could we want?

Walking in the Spirit

Trusty Radio

Turn the radio on and you get music or talk shows. The airwaves are full of sound even when we're not listening. There's *always* something on. We just have to tune in.

Tuning in to the radio is like walking with the Spirit. He's always there! The key is to "tune in" and pay attention. If he's always with us, with all his gifts and help, it's just smart to tune in. How *do* we tune in, respond to the Spirit's work in our lives, and give ourselves into his hands?

Get Sensitized!

We listen. The Holy Spirit is gentle. He respects our right to make our own choices. He never forces us. Because he speaks quietly, it's easier to hear him when *we're* quiet on the inside. That gets easier the more we understand that God's love is a solid rock. As we trust God, we give the noise of our worries, fears, complaints, and wants to him. We become quiet, knowing he's looking after it all. His peace fills us, and it's easier to hear the Spirit telling us what to do. We become aware of his quiet prompting—and we follow.

This inside quietness spreads through our lives. With God's help we keep our spirits and minds prayerful as we go through life, talk with someone, make a decision, do a chore, or play. We know God is constantly with us, and we *expect* the Spirit to be involved in our lives. It's like turning on that radio. Wherever we are, he's on the air with advice, understanding, and love!

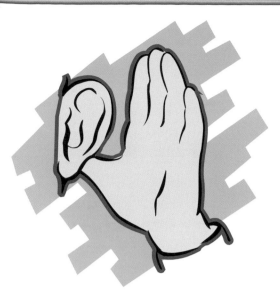

Listen and Act

It all starts with our relationship with God. We pray for help to be aware of him and be sensitive to the Spirit so we won't miss anything. Then, when we're chatting with a friend after school, we notice he's sad. In our hearts, we quietly ask God what to do. Then we get the courage to talk to our friend and ask how we can help.

Perhaps we're walking to the store and see a lady with lots of bags and a baby carriage. We feel a nudge to help her. Later we discover she had a lousy day and just asked God for help if he was real. Wow!

Or you're sitting at the supper table and everyone's talking. You notice your dad is tired and offer to pray for him. He's encouraged. On it goes.

Our job is to keep praying for more of God. And to continue obeying and loving God and

being sensitive to the Spirit. Life gets really interesting when we listen to God!

Prayer

This all works by prayer. That's how we build our relationship with God, getting to know him and what he wants. Through prayer we recognize the Spirit's leading. Take this example. A stranger calls. You don't recognize his voice. He says, "Come to the corner. I have something for you." You'd probably stay home. But if it was a good friend, you'd recognize his voice and off you'd go!

We have to talk to God enough to recognize him. Then, when he tells us to pray for someone or be kind to our sister because she's sad, we will. When we ask for the Holy Spirit to lead us and expect him to, he does. Guaranteed!

Bits 'n' Pieces

There's *lots* of stuff to know about the Holy Spirit. Here are a few more tidbits.

Q Can Christians hear God talking to them?

A In the Bible we read about people hearing God's voice. Today, the main way God speaks to us is through the Bible. That's why it's called "God's Word"—the Bible is God's message to us. God may also speak to us through people and circumstances and in other ways. But God will never tell us to do something that goes against what he says in the Bible. And don't forget, God is with us all the time through his Spirit.

Q Why do we pray?

A Prayer is talking with God. When we have a good friend, we talk to that person about all sorts of things. That's part of being a friend. In the same way, we should talk to God about what's happening in our lives. God wants us to share our lives with him, to tell him what makes us happy, sad, and afraid. He wants to know what we want and what we would like him to do, for ourselves and others. Also, when we pray, we open ourselves up to God so that his Spirit can make good changes in us.

Adapted from *101 Questions Children Ask About God*, Livingstone Corporation and Lightwave Publishing, 1992 and *103 Questions Children Ask About Right from Wrong*, Tyndale House Publishers, Inc. 1995. Used by permission.

Q How do I become even closer to God than I am now?

A Think of God as someone who wants to be your very close friend. For that to happen, you'll need to spend time together. You can spend time with God by reading his Word, the Bible. Ask your parents to help you know where and how to read. Also, talk with God about your life. Tell him you're sorry for disobeying him, and ask him to help you to get closer to him and do what he wants. You can also tell him about other people and their problems, asking him to help them.

You also get closer to God through worship. That's why churches have worship services. There, with other Christians, you can sing praises to God, talk to him, think about him, remember how much he loves you and what Jesus did for you, and learn from his Word.

Remember, God's Spirit will draw closer to you if you draw closer to God. Tell him you want to get to know him better. You can't get closer to God just by doing a few "Christian" things. But you can get closer by having a relationship with him!

Q Why do I feel afraid even though the Holy Spirit is with me?

A The Holy Spirit is always with us even though we don't see him and often we don't feel any different. He wants us to learn to trust him, to believe and know that he is there. It's natural to feel afraid. In fact, being afraid can be good. We should be afraid of danger. For example, fear can keep us a safe distance from a mean dog or something else that might hurt us. God wants our fears to remind us to trust him. Being afraid should be a signal to trust God and do what he wants us to do. But it doesn't mean that the Holy Spirit isn't with us.

Oh, What a Life!

We're born as little babies. We learn to walk, talk, take care of ourselves, get along with people, read, write, do math and chores, and more. In fact, we never stop learning! It's the same with God. We're born as Christians, discover who God is, and learn to walk and talk with him. We learn to love others, read and study the Bible, recognize God's gifts, and more. We just keep growing.

It's an adventure! Think of a kid who's just learning to walk. He can't imagine the things you've learned. Nor can you imagine what God has in store for you! Along the way the Spirit's fruit sprouts all over your life. You use the talents God has given you. And you pass on the Holy Spirit's gifts so others are encouraged and healed!

It's natural! There's nothing weird about God's work in our lives. Supernatural, yes, but then he's supernatural! He leads us and helps us do things no one can do alone. We're God's children. Why shouldn't we have supernatural lives from our supernatural Father? It's a natural part of being God's child!

It's a fact! The more we know God, the more sure we are of his love. As a result, we trust him more and follow his lead—even when he feels far away. Is he? No way! "Nothing at all can ever separate us from God's love because of what Christ Jesus our Lord has done" (Romans 8:39).

It's fun! Following the Holy Spirit is like an amazing roller coaster ride. We know something exciting is around the corner, but we're not sure what. God knows. His Spirit gets us ready. We believe, trust, and *go for it!*